Praise for *There Was Always Enough Time*

"Lorraine Lener-Ciancio's poems invite us to linger in her world briefly as she ponders love, loss, hunger, age, and longing. She makes it all seem like a comforting, knowable place. It's as though we inhabit these spaces of hers ourselves, smelling the ocean waves, tasting the chocolates, seeing the single snowflake in a beloved's hair, hearing jazz on the radio late at night, and remembering—what? that love endures...Tender understanding of the ravages of love and the passage of time is alive in the lines of her poems. The imagery is strangely sensuous, her truth-telling often stark and heartbreaking, her voice so clear. This evocative collection reminds us that there is reason to hope and dream in this life and that "there was always enough time.""

— Mag Dimond, author of
Bowing to Elephants; Tales of a Travel Junkie

"In this collection Lorraine Lener-Ciancio's smoothly lyric voice brings together precise descriptions of place with poems that glow like hearth fires, wrapping the reader in a soft and familiar warmth like a home-knit shawl.'

—Anne McNaughton, co-founder of Taos Poetry Bout

"*There Was Always Enough Time* is a time travelers document of places, emotions, memories of the senses. Here is a poet who is present in her life and charged with it. "...a remarkable kind of consonance.""

—Alan Macrae, author of *Mud, Space, and Spirit*

There Was Always Enough Time

Editor: Judyth Hill
Book and Cover Design: Mary M Meade
Author photo: Barry Silverstein
All other photographs: Lorraine Lener-Ciancio

Library of Congress Control Number: 2022931106

ISBN 978-1-7378109-1-9

There Was Always Enough Time

poems

Lorraine Lener-Ciancio

NIGHTHAWK PRESS
TAOS, NEW MEXICO

For Dante & Savannah
into the future

&

Barry
my present

CONTENTS

I.

II.

III.

IV.

I.

"Time is a foolish fancy, time and fool"

—DYLAN THOMAS

My Hands

"time strays into photographs and stops"
—*Anne Carson*

hold a camera
observe   pull back
lens between me & the world
drama   or drown in a river
of craving or elation

required & unrequited loves
nearly visible stretch of future
so carelessly consumed

when storms come
I'll pack my bag   return
when the sun comes out again
wind stops   safety overrated

I want the susurration & power
a force greater than me
a constant rhythm that follows

breath   heartbeat   nights awake
or soothed in a cradle
endlessly rocking
as the old poet said
a long time ago

Applied Life

Life, which had seemed so vast, is a
tinier thing than your handkerchief
—*Eugenio Montale*

So vast,

when sipping a glass of chilled white wine on a city
roof garden far from home & reading Montale alone
or trying to pry out a gnarly lavender bush from
my garden or slash at unyielding creosote,
nasty burrs adhere to my clothes.

So vast,

when making the bed, finding bits of melted chocolate
on the comforter from where we shared it last night
or watching a movie based on a song (that couple
who didn't get together until the very end), I know
my journey needs motionless moments & blurs of
brief joy, silences, even desolation.

    (riffles of air stir at the edge of my body
    a sound-producing organ—
    my soundtrack still playing
    after seven decades)
—when discovering there's always
another side to the record, another
poem in a book I thought already read—

So vast!

Distractibaking on
an April Morning 2020

and maybe it's not even morning anymore

or April

We turn heat up a notch
where it was before magnolia
trees bloomed pink under yesterday's
warm blue sky after we heard about
a Jersey family of eleven who lost
four adults in one day.

They say pollution's down in cities
—few vehicles on ten empty lanes
in L.A. & no traffic in Manhattan.
Elmo's gone from Times Square,
you can't call an Uber & my long
hair's white roots grow out.

We bake, use up overripe fruit
forgotten in bowls. Scent of banana
bread & sugar fills the kitchen as if
we were ready for guests to arrive
& not our possible lonely deaths
—two coffee cups left on the table.

Evening Late May:
Quarantine Dilemma or Gift

There are no myths here. It's dusk. Tall trees profuse with
new green, vodka & ice in a French Picardie tumbler. You sit
at the patio table on a chair cushion from a Pier One recently
closed down. Note the design echoes the leaves overhead.
It's all pleasant New Jersey backyard. Bare feet press into
thick spring grass as you put down your notebook & listen
to a cardinal emphatically trill goodnight notes from the
tallest branch & a neighbor across paths talks to someone
who laughs louder-than-natural. Distant warning whistles
sound as trains to & from Hoboken cross the road nearby.
The plenteous yard is lush, cool before summer heat comes
on with fireflies & cicadas, languid days, dried up gardens
that even sprinklers from Home Depot can't rescue by August.
Stirring breezes on newly bared arms portend rain later—
splendid for new evergreens. You would like to enter a fabled
green forest remembered from a book you read as a teen &
barely recall—only some of it—cool forests & a mysterious girl.
In your edited version (you tend to edit memory & experience)
you carry a Hermione wand & have learned a few incantations
intended to disappear too-close houses, too many cars in
driveways, lawn mowers that shatter calm, and trains. Always
the trains. Newly opened red roses look black in descending
dark as you step toward the house. Admit you like the yard at
dusk alone, then later a movie binge long past midnight cozy
with him. Laughing.

what if you can't stop
dreaming of another place
blue sky over wild columbine

Wonder Woman Does the Dishes:
A Suburban Pastoral

Une matinee, couverte en Juillet
Des ciels gris de cristal
—Rimbaud

an overcast morning in July with
crystal-gray skies   birds silent
by noon on a hot Saturday

a small girl across the path complains
her mother says she can't handle it
and you remember long ago impatience
desire to flee   yet responsibility
remained intact then   often shaken

even now you know how to don
gold Bracelets of Submission
to save yourself
do the dishes   allegory for
emotional control   who gets to eat

who gets to absorb outside forces
or repel them with her body
       the bracelets
       submerged in suds

September Tangles

it was the music
it was the moon
season of a bamboo fountain
a town upstate in Spring
it was a single snowflake's
intricate pattern in his hair
under a streetlamp in Canada
rain that fell upon the desert
the colt kicking up dust

it was his voice unheard in an
astonishment of tenderness
long after the rain & music
stopped   it was his hands again
on my body & that unfinished
portrait left behind on a chair
split by one sharp ray
of morning sun.
            It was that & nothing else.

Zen At Work Before Times

She likes scent & sound of morning
in coffee shops as brew hisses in pots,
steam rises, scones bake. She brings notebook,
pen, a Blackwing pencil, all to a quiet table
meant to linger at with gentle hits of single-
shot caffeine energy & thoughts brilliant
or banal scribbled on creamy paper.

Barista artists' hearts & leaves float
picturesquely on latte foam—proof
of Zen impermanence demonstrated
with a first sip. She writes of wine,
cappuccino in Italy, strong espresso
con grappa at a high table,
an edible Napoleon in Paris.

It's chill she's learned, to carry around
as you walk, a paper takeout coffee cup
with the name of a trendy local shop
on it, a New Yorker black and white
canvas tote on her shoulder—a slim
volume of a friend's poems inside, a new
lipstick called Plum Dandy, a bit of cash,
maybe two twenties, and a dark chocolate
fondant for later at home in swift dusk.

She has everything she needs on a dreary
day in early November in the northeast
where she lives now, leaves still on trees
first snowstorm not yet predicted. It's
too soon to wish for April to rescue her
although she wrote about Tom Waits & his
November song & no one she knows looks
unhappy on Facebook today.

A Certain Neatness in an Untidy Year

Coffeepot's ready for morning
Mallomars and M&Ms gone
providing forced virtue.

Meteorological winter is upon us—a
handsome weather guy with good suits
and hair on late news informs us of this.

Oranges in a blue bowl
ripen with a sharp scent
forgotten lemons grow hard.

The neighbor with Parkinson's
rakes dead leaves slowly
in the dark December evening.

Odes

I like this green ink
maybe I'll write
great poems
with it
like Neruda
who wrote odes
about everything
in green ink
Suppose it's all
in the ink?
What a notion!
words of poems
embedded
within the liquid
movement
of the pen
releases them
onto paper
Somewhat like
Michelangelo's concept
of a figure already in the stone
artist's action releases it
What odes would I write?
ode to my red fountain pen
ode to the Italians who made it
ode to its gorgeous real gold nib
ode to the bottle of *inchiostro*
ode to William Powell

and Myrna Loy's
silk striped pajamas
(because I watched an
old movie last night)
ode to all silk pajamas
ode to words
ode to freedom
ode to the great master
who said
to his assistant
draw Antonio draw!

Iotas and Shreds

she leaves her fountain pen
at the restaurant

        she is a photographist
        of neurotic realism

in a chilly casita she slips her
feet into raspberry wool socks

        still wants Sulka pajamas
        in pale blue silk

a jolly boat is a light vessel for
sheltered waters useful to land
on different shores

        she painted landscapes on
        tea bags & spider webs

in bed she tried to feel if it had
snowed during the night

        I won't dream about you
        she lied to her lover

he worked by light of stars alone
Mahler on the stereo

        a blue glass bottle shatters
        into sky shard pieces for him

by day ten she began
to go native

        sodden books   mildewed sofa
        soft green light of that dream

a half-knitted sock in a sack
eaten by a moth made
her weep for the moth

                                        she returned on a snowy night
                                        a blizzard in the canyon
                                        she was too late

the poet wore all sorts of purple
once survived sleep outside
in snowfall   died anyway

a squall is not a storm
a nor'easter is not a squall

she joins an opera company
gets to sing *amami* to Alfredo

she stole the image of fucking
James Dean in a meadow

a Buddhist monk drank
tequila & played blackjack
at their kitchen table

how many things concur
to keep a woman
from wandering

A Net Full of Disparate Catches
on the Atlantic Shore

Timeless sea breezes,
Sea-wind of the night
You come for no one...
—*Rilke*

bag of handmade chocolates
in gold paper from Third Avenue
Chocolate Shoppe, an open
Soaked in Crimson lipstick,
eyeglasses in a small pile of
tumbled-in-ocean-tides stones,
bleached and broken shells
—my writing table early
morning in a hotel room
overlooking an ocean

view of empty boardwalk
steel-blue waves borrowed for junctures
of words that might form a poem as
low tide exposes black rock breakwater—
window opened wide to hear the crash

—mind moves to rhythms
      pen scratch
           chocolate scent
              wind
       a laughing gull's raucous call

as I try to pull up from the deep sea
lyric nets of phrase   place them on
notebook pages with melodies   so you
understand why   I had to leave

II.

"And send us, lashed across choppy waters

and spilled drinks..."

—ARTHUR RIMBAUD

In Fullness of Time: A Romance

It's a story about snowy nights
his lake house at a forest's edge
blue bulbs in a bedroom lamp
illuminated sketches taped on walls
—a woman's face—
the one who left him years before—
words flared onto sheets of paper
the emblems of lone Decembers
—until you came along scented
with poems & family & warmth.

A radio station played all night long
soft songs from 60's & 70's—as we
touched, swallowed each other, learned
new landscapes of bodies & swam
in seas of intoxication—drunk
on perfect romance.

There was a midnight in another
place, tangled in all thirty-five years
—when we damaged love
still connected to shadows in the night
and not each other.

Meet Me

in Rome at Harry's Bar in 1979
on a hot August evening   our
hunger new & us afraid
if we stayed too long we would miss
the last train to Ostia

at their tables   at the bar
strangers recognized
we were everything new
& perfect to each other flushed
with summer & sex & beauty

there were terrifying angels astir
in watercolor light   wings that
altered perception on busy streets
as the substance of our future
changed   old ties broken
new ones born   in soft air

meet me in 1979 at the hotel
whose name I cannot remember
near black sand beaches with
heavyset *nonas* lugging pots
of macaroni across hot sand

the café with tables in the street
where I ordered *fritto misto*
& didn't know there would be
tentacles in it & we laughed

meet me right there on that night
of tentacles   give me again
a polished green-tinted shell
the old woman gave you for me
looked us over   sighed dramatically
       ah amore

did you still have it somewhere
in our home that last snowy night
in February? I never found it
and I looked everywhere

Celestial Navigation, 1988

The night nurse's name was Jim.
He sat by your bedside with a hair dryer
blew hot air onto a seventh bag of frozen blood.

You talked of astronomy, the cosmos,
—he was studying celestial navigation.
You confessed you sometimes longed to travel
in space, leave cold grays of grim winter
arrive at distant universes.

Slow-moving changes came over you after.
You heard distant hum of trains & grew wistful,
summer nights made you sad.

You dreamt of an old love, what went wrong,
called her, learn she is retired, lives at the edge
of a golf course in Arizona. Wonder if in a
parallel life you would play golf together on a
morning lawn, picturesque swans in a nearby pond
—remember you don't like golf.

You lost most of your blood back then,
weren't expected to live. Left the hospital
cheeks flushed with blood of others—new
best friends you hadn't met & never got to love.

You kept a knife under your pillow the
first night home. Dreamt about your brother's
salmon pink Bel Air convertible from thirty
years before & the woman you loved now—how
her sweater worn those nights at your bedside in
the chilly room was the color of blood.

Manuscript Notes and Blue Moons

At first you couldn't tell us apart. Old vows held fast even as rocks tumbled around us careening down mountainsides. Hills collapsed, apricot blossoms froze in spring. All that remained was the small lamp over his bed at the end of February as snow fell silently into the night and a pale-yellow light spilled onto his face. Maybe it was the color his skin had taken on. I couldn't tell. I hadn't seen him in a while & now I'd arrived a little too late. That whole end of winter, early spring, I cleared out the house that was ours. It stood empty for two years. Rooms echoed with the silence of tall ceilings, of walls without art or photographs. I worry something is left behind, abandoned. There was that one blue door he'd lost the key for. It might have been filled with scenery, costumes, backdrops, my old red sweater.

lights went down
—our long run over
the stage empty

∽

I sold his expensive fly-fishing rod, the one I'd bought for $300 & gave him because he dreamed of fishing in the Rio Grande. I sold it to the elderly Taoseño for $10. He'd returned several times, looked at it longingly, touched it gently as if it were a woman's arm. He couldn't afford the $125 estate sale price. As he carried it away, he said he would use it to catch dinner for himself and his family—that it was the right time of the year now, the river would soon be filled with rainbow trout—*big ones*. He would teach his grandkids how to cast into the great *Rio*, not just look at it & dream over it the way Anglo artists and poets usually did.

don't fall in love with a dreamer

he breathed himself into
torments
of shadows

I left to seek light

he went
where there is no light at all
and stayed

evening of my last walk
I said farewell through misty eyes
goodbye mountains, lavender sky,
breezes, magpies, horses in the field
I'm feeling melancholy tonight
I told them when their car stopped
on the dirt road to ask after me—
he reached over to clasp my hand

I had a home in Des Montes at the foothills of the Rockies. The winds from the west brought echoes of ancient seas, scent of salt that lingered across mesas, canyons. Monsoon winds blew around our tall house in July & carried voices of the ancestors. They weren't our ancestors, but I honored them. The morning air came tinged with coral light as sun rose over eastern peaks and filled the bedroom. Sun always felt warm even in January & all through the winter. Nights cold all summer long; bitter toe-biting chill on winter nights when air pierced lungs with crystal clear cold & perfume of piñon & cedar smoke emanated from chimneys of kiva fireplaces & wood stoves in town. From my many-windowed house I saw cloaks of fragrant smoke settled over the valley, softening crisp moonlight by night & bright sun by day. We had a home in that runic place for three decades, watched & counted hundreds of Full Moons golden, white, blue, rise over the Sangre de Cristos. And then one more night and then one more night and then... a deep darkness that was always there waiting....

Windswept November

Late afternoon, candles, tea.
She writes two pages, notices
rhododendron's tight winter buds,
gradual snow-covered limbs

hears invisible sparrows
suffuse cold air with leafy hedge
symphonies.

Her eyes close over the notebook,
drift into weightless dreams
of the deep snow she knows
has fallen where he is.

Misty vision of a *composanto*—
under white, a plaque with his name
faded. Walmart plastic angels' wings of
colors that change in sun & wind's touch.

Alone in death, always alone,
—*even with someone he loved*—
a desperado's nom de plume tomb,
no art fills an empty studio.

Out of dream-space she scans the quiet room—
candle flame still shimmers in descending dark,
his paintings hang on a wall & she feels
snow-laden pines, remembers how
together, the heat, without warning,
began to diminish.

Writ Large

He was dancing to some music
no one else had ever heard
—Harry Chapin

You had to write him large
—the size of your words
obliterated his shadows.

You had to create him a little
larger than he was & dispel
clouds of despair in his eyes.

You didn't ask where
his defeat came from &
you still write him large

—his dance with death
that night when the moon
waxed crescent in Pisces &
snow fell in the canyon

—the sacred mountain &
all it represented to him was
hidden behind the cold white
whispers of his last dream

he'd told you about a man who
collected stars in a jar & wanted
someone to watch over them
when he was gone. And you became,
that night, the keeper of his stars.

III.

"I just wanted a place to wait on the moon"

—Po Chu-i, (772-846)

Now It's a New Season

April rescued you
from winter   tiny pink
petals blew past
east coast windows
on spring breezes

window   windrift   weep
over deep purple lilacs
that bloom now
against an adobe wall
you somehow lost

fragrances scattered   dissipated
wasted on mountain winds
as you lean against a blue doorway
in your mind—color of sky
when lilacs bloom in an exact
place you will never again
lean into.

Wednesday Morning Writers
in an Earthship Zendo

(for N.G.)

notebooks once pristine
display pages with curled corners
puckered by 69 gallons of tears
84 delusions   memories   searing rage
smeared ink   unpunctuated sentences

fathers abound in these books
if not in the room   the good ones   the bad
mothers can't be resolved anymore
maybe fathers can
& everyone needs a grandmother

there's a favorite aunt   deceased ex-husbands
former lovers growing old at a distance
elephants   leaky rowboats
cars that didn't start twenty years ago
city gardens of yellow chrysanthemums
acres of identical gray gravestones under a bridge

pages grow dense with ordinary things
meals   visions of summer salads   a wine
so exquisite that its name was forgotten
in the taste-budded bliss that followed
mourning that won't stop   guilt
on mornings that pass too quickly
fear of spiders large enough to have elbows

uncommon days feel golden or violet-gray
someone senses autumn in the air

another could believe he's on a tropical island
but we are all just in an adobe Earthship

gazed upon by Zen masters in photos and
statues of poets who died in the 12th century
river rocks   incense   candle flame
a steadfast mountain outside the window

silent—we step out the door
pens capped   cushions brushed off
ink-spillers avoid looking at each other
until a chance meeting in town occurs
rife with abundant understanding
      we know we haven't told it all

At a Friend's House in Santa Fe While She Travels

Alone I drove down, brought my pillow,
a blanket I'd knitted with yarn scraps,
too many books, pens, notebooks.

She invited me to sleep in her bed—
Pendleton blanket, stuffed animals,
morning sun on my hair to wake me
as birds chattered in aspens just outside.

How precisely light came through
the open door into my cup of tea,
a plate with bits of egg yolk on it,
clear air outside & a rabbit in the
garden.

There were blossoms I cut & placed
in a chipped tea mug already
fading after one day... awareness
of fragility, things that bloom &
die in still-cold tricky spring—just
as you begin to notice.

What it Once Was by
Narragansett Bay

midnight at a timeworn oak table
in a hundred-year-old kitchen

bouquet of wild white daisies
in a cracked pitcher

a notebook   a pen
—a cat named dirty harry
sits in a window under
softly tinkling glass chimes

you touch tea-stain silk ribbons
sure the old woman's spirit left
them for you to find in the dusty
closet under the steps

breezes from nearby bay carry
plangent foghorn sounds onto
cursive inky scrawls on curled pages
as you write these words....

you dreamt long after of a walk
toward the house   tall pine trees
pre-hurricane   still there

your hair was on fire & the
pages of your blue notebook
were empty

A Long Winter of Discontent in Four Parts

for Gayle

I.

I jotted observations & cautions in a notebook from a comfortable perch in a white wicker chair   didn't write about the nasty bits or her painted toenails grown so long she called them vampire nails or how we laughed together & I hoped she wouldn't ask me to cut & polish them. Instead, I knitted socks during those weeks & months—a sort of yarn diary. Yarn colors represented moments in time, bright jewels of autumn, greens of eventual spring. The dalmatian warm at my feet echoed black & white wools. I sat by the bedside, witness to severe winter in the mountains that year, a sudden March thaw, muddy roads frozen & unfrozen, how the moon waxed full on her last night & a far off drumming suffused the chill wind as I drove home. She didn't wear the socks I made, liked the colors & silence that wove them together but not the stitch bumps. I told her she was the princess & the pea. She appreciated that in the story the princess sleeps on a soft bed with prince charming & lives forever.

full cold rays of light
stream into kitchen windows
first moon of new spring

II.

finches chirp excitedly in bare trees
feathers not yet resplendent
but with excitement
—in false spring

tethered leaves cling to indifferent branches
until they resemble Calder mobiles
art sent from the gods   she said

moments when we care
about nothing   hold hands
should I go home now?
no   stay   and I do
bring tea   diced peaches on
a white plate   linen napkin

we didn't know we would never
discuss regret again or that
I would stop at the door closed
against fractured winter...

no regrets?   could I say it?
we kept terror away   until
her words swept us in
as the collector knocked...

...witness me pack up cut lilies
& a last bit of ruined perfume
lingered   in the
pierced cold air

III.

this I know
people write poems
when someone they love dies
the long lead up to it
unbidden memories
altered in dreams

five friends on our beach
my emerald-green bathing suit
worn at thirty   how she envied
my tan set off by vibrant color
"like a painting" she visualized
she would one day make

faraway look in her eyes
the day when in faded jeans
of the kind we all wore to march
in protest of an immoral war &
she said let's go away to Colorado

we were Atlantic babes
Manhattan wannabe's in a
Connecticut town—out there
they wore blue jewelry

we stayed   sat in a circle of five
on our sandy beach   best friends
as kids interrupted the bitching
asked for ice pops   hot dog   taffy

...we didn't go   any of us   not then
because we couldn't leave
even though our lovers called us
and the future looked exciting

IV.

In my bed in red flannel
pajama pants printed with
cartoon dogs & stars
I dreamt of her bed empty
as someone removed
sheets & pillows

I swept the floor
with a twig broom as
white down feathers
gathered in a pile
until they scattered

remembered something
I wanted to tell her
but didn't & now
it was too late
all I had were
scattered memories
& an inadequate broom

Last Lightening

It was unusually warm for March that
day when winter broke for a while
   wind at last quiet.

The long relentless snow season
of your slow dying at last over,
mud still frozen, night different...

You lay under an L.L. Bean comforter
wearing a new nightgown. Your husband
and daughter knew you liked to look good
when company was expected.

I stood alone near your bed
where days had passed for us—
me knitting, writing, long weeks
as doula to your decline.

You said you liked it
—the silence
—the industry
we didn't talk much.

Now I wanted to know how chill distance felt,
ask is it true there is no time & space?
       —tell me now!

I wanted answers you wouldn't give
& my presence went unacknowledged.

Two men whose names we didn't ask
gently placed a thin red blanket
on your chilled body. I worried you'd be cold
or annoyed by that color you never wore.

The Skyless Sky

for Ted

The light
was without light, the sky skyless
—Pablo Neruda

This morning half-awake I recall
you appeared in my dream
leaned against a wall
wearing a khaki jacket
kept cleaned & pressed
like all your understated smart clothes
—you had that about you
blue cotton shirts, creased jeans,
soft leather loafers.

You looked straight into my eyes.
I thought you would speak but you didn't.
It seemed you had a message to deliver.
All I could think of, seeing that you'd died
more than two years ago, was that you would
be there for me when my end came &
maybe it was near or maybe you were a
free soul after that unexpected exit one day
before the Porsche finally arrived.

You were surely surprised, angry in that
other state of being. The one we joked
about the day we had lunch at the Mexican
café in Taos outside under the umbrella with
our new partners and the mountain: *last days,
age, last cars, death,* we talked for hours.
We didn't really believe it. Who does?

The image of you has lingered all day.
I'm still waiting for the message.
Did you want to tell me *every day is the best
day of your life—the best day...*
you said things like that as you got older.

IV.

"Stars... Little centuries opening

just long enough for us to slip through"

—OCEAN VUONG

Sirens Break Hearts

Don't think, you who do not know, old lovers
are finished. It still burns & undoes us
in full fragrance, bloom & touch.

Because of what came before we have no need
to see if we are compatible. Darkness has
no influence in a synchronicity
of having found each other anew.

Words are filled with experience,
pain, samsara, sadness, desire.
What voice tells us? What ear hears us?

We scale ramparts as rain pelts
against doors we reach, knock upon
awash, shivering. Ignore reality to seek

what was lost, arms we could not feel,
close distances unimaginable. We do not ask
permission to enter, dismiss 3a.m. fears,
rain—in our songs and my name.

This time of life there are diamonds, no rust.
Hear deep sound? Nina Simone, lilac wine.
Chet Baker falling in love too easily. Can
almost hear the hush of bare feet on wood floors
far away scent of cool wind in clouds.
It's high tide now where he is.

A Bronx Tale

Write about the boy in the south Bronx who stepped over fighting men on the subway station's platform to see his girlfriend in the north Bronx. How far he walked, how fearless or foolish he was and how it left him unharmed with stories to tell. Write about the night he walked from his girl's house, not to the subway, but toward your house because even in two brief histories something had already unalterably shifted. Write about how he lost his courage and the boy and girl were kept apart by tricky goddesses and divergent destinations and how the universe made them wait until the man could tell the woman the story fifty years later, his lips to her ear, his hand near her heart—a whisper

last night
tonight
will be like
future nights

Pot of Basil

all day and night, music
—*Rumi*

I want to bring a pot of basil
to your front steps

buy you a blue shirt
& flutes for the dance

—a bottle of French wine
expensive Provençal rosé

drink it all tonight because
it is still summer & intoxicating

scent of basil   table in the yard
wine glasses too delicate for outside

candles flare up   burn low
the wine bottle is empty

we make plans we may keep
this time

It Was the Way

angels of flame and ice
little eve of drunkenness, help!
—*Rimbaud*

it all came together,
a few words—*some things*
never change & constellations
of hearts blew open in ways
unimagined during years
of desire turned to ash.

It was the way
summer passed into autumn
first snow on peaks, awareness
of summer lives long gone,
what came next would happen
in a clutter of brief stars
on cold winter nights.

It was the way longing, desire
slid into fantasies of moonlight, dance,
red wine, new words of undead passion
—in three languages. What kept us apart
still kept us apart, but you caught my heart
off guard. There is no turning back
when the unknowable is in motion.

Harvest Moon

there's a full moon rising
let's go dancing in the light
—*Neil Young*

When we speak again
please tell me how I looked
on that day when I said let's
do it again, meaning, all of it
the loving, the decisions reversed
but not the dissembling. Please
tell me again how we tried to be
free in that city on a March
afternoon when we were lost
in an urban park. Tell me.

How did I look? Did we really
hold hands the whole time?
Did I wear that 1970's shiny coat
& high heels? Dark hair straight?
Please tell me if you remember
that room on the other side
of the George Washington Bridge
a few hours on a summer afternoon
Dan Hicks & The Hot Licks
on the static-y radio.

Please tell me now
how you felt our hearts
burst open without warning
two old lovers who met again
longed to dance in the full moon's light
seek what was lost to find more
than imagination made possible.
Remind me again how it feels
to enter spaces where nothing
has failed.

Crazy Has Places to Hide In

—Leonard Cohen

In a village nearby Holy Trinity's bell
rings sharp against cold cobalt sky
as we glide between seasons
last days of autumn used up.

We create, undo, give meaning
to everything—just to feel joy
after winter winds subside
or later when lilacs bloom
purple behind city walls.

In this complicated while
of letting go, holding on,
snow continues to fall.

500 Cellphone Minutes

Phone calls from the only place to pick
up a signal—post office parking lot—
with you at your house 2,000 miles away
thick book on your lap, jazz from speakers
a movie on the coffee table for later alone.

Your old computer sends new verses you compose
for me devised from song lyrics, musings, longings
wistful thirsty laments, lusts, recollections, hopes.

We wait for the time when actual distance
will be diminished. I read Rilke's letters, tell you
about his lover Lou, but you already knew—
I want to be her to *my* poetry man. You want

me to be me, say YOU in capital letters.
When we stop endless talk, use up many minutes,
I carry my joy quietly.

Recall that you said walks
in winter woods—you know just the places
how you want to reach over to touch me
in the night, be in the time that comes after.

Every spirit has a voice. I hear yours singing
inside of me—a remarkable kind of consonance.

What Has Survived Another Winter?

to all the poets of my heart

You are compelled to answer
      splendidly
with ancient poet's words:

I want to set my life on fire
seek the one who fans the flames
find what you love and let it kill you
              —Rumi

        500 lyrics of romantic songs
        500 minutes on a cellphone
        too many notebooks
        crows on a wire
        robins too early in February
        an older woman's selfies
        —with make-up
            & a ring light

You have come too far now to turn back he says,
she answers, I won't let you go ever again.
They look toward brighter light...an end of dukkha
the signal to come home to the limit of life
& still she ponders luxurious suffering...

        limited cellphone minutes &
        advice from Elizabeth Taylor:
        pour yourself a drink, put on some lipstick
        (preferably crimson)
        and pull yourself together

Sometimes the future slaps you in the face
reaches out with loving arms.

It's all about universal timing
—whatever the cause
we are now in this fine madness together
we have survived another winter.

Mercury's Direct Again

The soundtrack has changed
from Diamonds and Rust to
Losing My Mind. River of Coltrane's
sensual sax flows down that Long
Winding Road & under a Harvest Moon—
to celebrate, see its light in your eyes—
when he tells me love is the joy
love is the glory I know he's
gone mad, too. I'll raise funds
for hurricane victims tomorrow.
For now, all reason, scholarship
civil disobedience   poetry
has turned toward the one
who found me again.

August Night, Raining

it's always raining in this song
—David Duchovny

hidden mist-shrouded
mountains of feelings
I want   I want

he sings in my ear
my one and only love
why are you the one

out of all the others
he asks   is this
our personal

American tragedy
a broken fairy tale
or destined to be

better than before
& briefer
here's looking at you kid

Maybe I Am

not the woman you think I am
not one of the ladies who lunch
nor the homemaker who dusts
cooks dinner, tosses off her apron
& is dynamite in the sack wearing
black satin & ribbons—although
that is an option

I am & will be your lover as time unwinds
I am the woman you call smart   a little crazy
I am the woman who will provoke you
expand the limits of your life & love
    —you say I already have
I am the woman you can't pin down
except sometimes when I want you to

maybe I will
choose a book of poems over parties
cross a river in a paddleboat with you
walk barefoot upon the sand and
climb 217 steps up the lighthouse
let you examine every inch of me
be your driver   climb inside   I'll
bake you a sugar cake
        —with extra frosting
to eat in bed...

I am the woman who
      always loved you

Moonstruck

Here I am. I stand before you
not a young woman—the one
you remembered—nor middle-aged.
My flesh is not firm & I do
feel bad about my neck.
But my bare skin is warm.

What is age to moonstruck
lunatics? Let the sane people
eat their hearts out.
We accept yes as the answer.

One Late Morning

Madness does this—
sends your pen places
to find your authentic self
recall men who loved you
the ones you loved

The day he found you again—one
you'd let go of in whose arms
there is a last home in the now—
one more bead strung on life's necklace
with silk cord & thorns   He beckoned
you walked in between swords

Forever is like this today—
a white breakfast plate
cup of jasmine tea   egg shells
one red maple leaf that slowly
descends past the window

From Pebbles to Duende at Sunset

what about that red leather handbag you didn't buy
photographs of sunsets you forgot to print

the sweater you like a lot but can't find &
where did the authentic turquoise necklace go?

do you need the Mason jar filled with imperfect
shells from that first trip down the shore where

everything is alright & he said you're a Jersey Girl
now & played Springsteen singing it

or the amethyst geode & handful of pebbles from
Sunset Beach on the Delaware where you thought

signs read *no launching of witchcraft* & you
learned that pebbles in the sand when polished

sparkle like real diamonds   You think this *is* a form
of witchcraft   maybe the signs were literal after all

he gave you a silver heart on a chain embedded
with a beach diamond he said would last forever

you'd heard that one before   forever
this time you believe it   conjuration is astir

Day 100: NJ

leopard print panties
silky & lace-trimmed
slow turns of ceiling fan
a cardinal's trill outside
an opened window
Harvest Moon soon

You're waxing full in
breeze-sweet nights of dark
chocolate & moon's
gleam to dance in the light of
barefoot in a suburban yard
on cool grass

Gradual wonders clear doubts
as another season passes
an embrace of mornings
nights in warm arms with no
hesitation   no hidden secrets
or darkness

You finally emerge from old-snow
feelings into glass-green sea   color
you wanted your eyes to be—like your
mother's—you didn't know that until
this clear-now

Feels Like Home

feels like I'm on my way back
to where I come from
—Randy Newman

Pour chilled Pinot Grigio over three raspberries
in the glass with the tall stem. Note how light glints
in the wine. Take a picture of it & lush green
grass on a late April day after rain   finally
warm enough to be outside at a table under
old pine trees. So green it's like Ireland—
what you saw of it long ago—a descending plane
over all sorts of green—proverbial patchwork like
here, now, improbable New Jersey!

You didn't leave the airport in Ireland to walk
verdant fields that one day while you waited with
your lover for a connection to Atlanta & bought
an Irish Fisherman's sweater hand knitted, tags
informed you, by Mary O'Donohue. In August,
Italy had been hot. You needed warmth in Shannon.
Your lover became your husband. You kept the
sweater for years—it felt like home when you wore it
until one day it was lost.

You eat the wine-soaked raspberries, move toward
the brick house you live in now. Sometimes
you love someone again who feels like home.
It makes you want to lose yourself.

Martini Thoughts with Notebook on a Hot Summer Afternoon

Looking at recipes
in a new cookbook:
rice-wine-braised chicken,
garam masala lamb patties.

I make a shopping list that
in a week will be a mystery
—a memory of inspiration
blown by summer winds.

I do note three olives
in the Tito's martini he
(a vegetarian) prepared for me
just the way I like it: dry, cool.

My headache is gone, the table
is strewn with twenty-four Crayola
colored pencils & pages with names
of poetically edible flowers:

hibiscus, pansies, borage, calendula,
nasturtiums, roses, sage, dandelion wine,
sugared violets—& a recipe for
lavender avocado pudding...

—not that I'll ever make it
but I wanted the recipe that
seemed oddly epic like pink sea salt
from the Red Sea I learn is
a seawater inlet of the Indian Ocean.

I'll never visit it except
with three olives
in a martini
he made for me
on a summer afternoon
on the screened-in
porch
in New Jersey.

There Was Always Enough Time

"there's only one way to smell a flower
but there's a million ways
to be free"
—David Byrne

—sweatshirts & clean smell   the way he
nods over a book & knows every lyric to
blues songs, every joke written before 1950
pleased I don't remember punch lines
no matter how often I hear them—
he doesn't get the blues in the night

I make green tea & bake fancy pear galettes
with demerara sugar sprinkled on top   buy
bouquets of daffodils in the market for the
February table—he said there were robins on
his walk yesterday—now they're in a poem

we haven't gotten to see northern lights yet
or lavender fields of Provence but I brought
him to my lost mountain & we watched an
August full moon rise over it like in a song
whose every lyric he knew

I know now there was always enough time
and the light in the dim room upstairs on
sweet afternoons isn't as bright as fires
that go on flaming within—it's almost
like a song

winter vanished
a calendar page slipped off
suddenly, spring

NOTES

"Time is a foolish fancy, time and fool" by Dylan Thomas, from his poem: *When, Like a Running Grave*

"Life, which had seemed so vast; is a tinier thing than a handkerchief" by Eugenio Montale, from *Otherwise,* translation: Jonathan Galassi

"time strays into photographs and stops" by Anne Carson, from *The Autobiography of Red*

"Une Matinee, couverte en Juillet; Des ciels gris de cristal" by Arthur Rimbaud, from *Fragments of Folio 12* in *Illuminations,* translation: "an overcast morning in July" by John Ashbery

"Timeless sea breezes; Sea-wind of the night; You came for no one..." by Rainer Maria Rilke, translation: Albert Ernest Fleming

"And send us, lashed across choppy waters and spilled drinks..." by Arthur Rimbaud, from *Illuminations* translation from French: John Ashbery

"He was dancing to some music no one else had ever heard" by Harry Chapin, song lyric from *Shooting Star*

"I just wanted a place to wait on the moon" by Po Chu-i (772-846) from poem: *Pondside,* translation: J.B. Seaton

"The light; was without light, the sky skyless" by Pablo Neruda, from poem *Horses,* translation: Alastair Reid

"Stars… Little centuries opening; just long enough for us to slip through" by Ocean Vuong, from *Night Sky With Exit Wounds*

"All day and night, music" by Rumi, translation: Coleman Barks

"angels of flame and ice; little eve of drunkenness, help" by Rimbaud, *Illuminations*, translation: John Ashbery

"there's a full moon rising; let's go dancing in the light" song lyric by Neil Young, from *Harvest Moon*

The title of poem *Crazy Has Places to Hide In* is borrowed from Leonard Cohen's song, "Crazy to Love You"

"I want to set my life on fire; seek the one who fans the flames; find what you love and let it kill you" by Rumi, translation: Coleman Barks

"It's always raining in this song" lyric by David Duchovny, from *The Rain Song*

"feels like I'm on my way back; to where I come from" Title & epigraph borrowed from *Feels Like Home* by Randy Newman

ACKNOWLEDGEMENTS

My thanks and love to poet and friend Phyllis Hotch who left us too soon at 93 years old, for taking first looks at these poems; to other accomplished poets and writers too numerous to mention who worked with and inspired me through the years. You know who you are. Gratitude for those gifted people who took time to read and blurb this collection. To my soul-sister Mag who read the first rough draft of the last section on a cold evening a few years ago, with wine, and encouraged me to continue. Gratitude to the women of the Manuscript Clan of 2020 who got me back on track. Many thanks, always, to SOMOS (Society of the Muse of the Southwest) for support in my writing, curating, and editing endeavors over many years, to various literary journals and anthologies where other poems appeared, to Adobe Walls for publishing "Odes" that reappears, slightly modified, in this collection. Special thanks to Mary Meade who designed this book from her world in Mexico and, of course, to Rebecca Lenzini, Nighthawk Press, for believing in me again. Always, heartfelt thanks to my partner Barry who somehow, every time, understands.

ABOUT THE AUTHOR

Lorraine Lener-Ciancio is the author of *From Salt to Sage,* stories from a zig-zag journey, a collection of personal essays and experiences of place, American-Italian identity, old and new love, east coast roots, from the Atlantic to the Southwest and back. (Nighthawk Press, 2017, Taos, NM). She has written feature articles for various magazines and art sections of weekly newspapers. Her poems and non-fiction have been published in anthologies and literary reviews. She was a featured writer in *Stitching Resistance: Women, Creativity, and Fiber Arts,* (Solis Press, England, 2014), and her photographs have appeared in books and often, covers, of other writers (see *Surviving the Winter* (UNM Press), as well as a variety of anthologies. Her story-essays appeared in two volumes of *Knit Lit* (Three Rivers Press, NYC). She was longtime editor of *Chokecherries*, an annual literary anthology from SOMOS (Society of the Muse of the Southwest), co-edited publications, *Storied Recipes* and *Storied Wheels* and curated Right to Write events sponsored by SOMOS & Pen America. She lives in northern New Jersey in a ninety-year-old house on a park, with her partner (also a writer) and a lot of books.

Made in the USA
Middletown, DE
23 April 2022

64642207R00052